in Sunshine And in Shadow

Dear Michele,

I hope you'll enjoy these!

in Sunshine *And in* Shadow

Beth Harry

To order additional copies of this book, contact:
Xlibris Corporation
1-888-795-4274
www.Xlibris.com
Orders@Xlibris.com
48220

in Sunshine *And in* Shadow

Beth Harry

To order additional copies of this book, contact:
Xlibris Corporation
1-888-795-4274
www.Xlibris.com
Orders@Xlibris.com
48220

Preface

I wrote these poems over a period of many years, publishing just a few in amateur journals and hoping that someday I would pull them all together. Coming finally to that point is a gesture of recognition and thanks for a life full of the joy and pain that come with love, and a deep sense of connection to the universe in all its dark and brilliant power. Growing up by the sea, in Little Bay, Port Maria, my senses were tuned to the midday "sun-hot" and the sound of the sea at night, rolling, I thought, right up under our house; to the taste and scent of salt-soaked almonds on the beach; and to the resonance of my father's deep baritone sliding easily from "*Old Man River,*" to "*Peanut Vendor,*" to "*Linstead Market*" and "*Mango Walk*". Through those sights and sounds I learned that life was the color of the Poinciana in bloom and that the sea rolled on no matter what. Later, through that same baritone, the words of "*Danny Boy*" came to comfort me when sunshine gave way to shadow. Today, I dedicate this collection of poems to Ben, who lights up my life.

Table of Contents

I: POINCIANA

II: OCEAN NIGHTS

III: EDEN

For Ben

Sudden in a shaft of sunlight
Even while the dust moves
There rises the hidden laughter
Of children in the foliage
Quick now, here, now, always—
Ridiculous the waste sad time
Stretching before and after

(T.S. Eliot, Four Quartets: Burnt Norton)

POINCIANA

poinciana

now
while there's salt and almond in the air
let me love my nakedness
and mesmerize you
sly chameleon
before you turn into the brownness
of your tree

if I can scratch that camouflage
I swear you'll live for me
while poinciana flames
on the sun-hot land
canonizing
the fast-burning
hallelujah years

Little-Bay (Port Maria)

those were the years when the mid-day warmth
stayed awake past sunset
when morning waves never littered the shore with broken boughs
when day-time tears were dried by the breath of evening breezes
and noon-hour doubts were banished by moonlight
on coconut husks

all through those years
the needle-like rocks beneath the sea-wall
befriended our feet
with the poignance of childish reproach
and painful affairs were as far from shore
as the reef at evening
when the tide rolls in and shelters
the coral-wrought submarine castles

but tides come and go with a force
that frightens the rocks
and today
there are newborn caves
in the walls of the bay

rainbows at seventeen

we walked in the sun
till the clouds took its place
and it rained

we walked in the rain
till the clouds grew old
then we laughed

we laughed through our fears
while the velvet sky grew blacker
but the moon was too cold
so we cried

we danced in a dream
till the dream collapsed
then we rested

we rested till dawn
but the dew was too wet
so we ran

we ran till we tripped
on the pot of gold
at a rainbow's end

but we knew we'd forget
how to cry
if we stayed
so we left

ecstasy

drifting
soaring
gliding
through a turquoise haze
of cloudless
windless
air

strands of silver
tie my fingers
to the moon
and raindrops
are entangled
in my hair

clinging to a rainbow
holding hands with every ocean
every stream

with you

touching fingertips
the horizon out of sight
and everest in miniature
below me

B

now

the child is me
racing between trees
climbing from limb to limb
punching holes
in the stem
to see
the sap
run out
fingers placed
to catch
the ooze
and joy
in the trickle

oh
this freedom-seeking
child

oh
you
my dream-lover

everything I own (version)

once
in an earlier incarnation
you said to me
  don't go
as I cut the cord and set me free

stretching
my young-girl
ska-time
wings of a dove
to fly the coop of love
with which you had encircled me

as I crossed the final border
of my childhood's territory
how could I know I would return
to say to you
(impossibly)
  don't go
 encircle me
 again

B'

renewal

climbing out of the wide, low river-bed
the narrow road winds
hugging the mountain-side

and I
clinging to the moment
absorb the greenness and fertility
of another time
another self
the valley's dampness on my skin
and you in my eyes

against the towering back-drop
of Mount Rosser
your face becomes my world
an image to imprint indelibly on my mind
an image of this fecund country-side
and you and I
trying to exhume from this rich soil
our childhood's dream

and then I know that what I want from you
is one more chance to celebrate
everything I left behind when I left you
the tortuous mountain road
the valley and the sky
the deep-down rhythm of the land
the buoyance of your smile

to hear Jamaica in your voice
to see Jamaica in your eyes

I never wrote poems

I never wrote poems
for you
before
because
before
with you
the things I had to say
were easy
rolling
like an infant's babble
off my childhood's tongue

no need then
for the enriched image
the sharp analogy
or convoluted metaphor
of adult eyes
the fluent
I-love-you of youth
sufficed

but now
I speak to you in unknown tongues
hoping to reveal through words' disguise
the soaring joy and sense of loss
I feel
at loving you again

animus

where did you learn
to love so easily
so simply
drawing
in sharp relief
the cut-off points
of love

while I tremble
in its aweful glow
mourning each tomorrow

love on ice

love on ice
a cool transparence
letting in the light

how easy now
to see
in crystal clarity
the clean-cut conformation
of a dream

eyes wide open
to discern
its wild and beautiful
impossibility

the dance: prologue

I play   the willing fly to your Anansi
watching
as you outline the intricate circles of your dance
                    each vortex rivaling the next
then calmly
cross   the interface with cool diagonals
                    fragile compass points
                    just sharp enough to wound
                    yet draw no blood
and so
I play   the knowing fly to your Arachne
noting   the angle of your shoulder
as you step aside   deftly innocent of the deed
side-step me   just in time
then
circle

I pause

hovering   in your wake
                                          unintimidated
                              by this precarious balance

                    one more of your imperious
            invitations
and I
so well
aware
            of my part in the play
will
            (oh baby!)
obey

                    B

Anansi/Br'Anancy: West African spider trickster hero

the dance: epilogue

I planned a poem, showing you, my fleet-footed trickster, after all your fancy footwork, chastened, for once not fast enough, as I, now nimble-fingered and above all, brave, with a quick flick of the wrist tug at a loose thread left dangling from your last circle

but you stole the poem and today, once more anticipating me, melted before my disbelieving eyes

and all at once I saw the impossibility of it all—the cool truth of this pretty affair—that if I put my body in your hands there'll be no more talk of webs and dances, no more players, no curtain, and no stage, and believe me love, no more applause

what then, my lord, when in your arms you find no clever courtesan, no dilettante at love, but instead the unpolished flesh and raw truth of my demanding womanhood?

sacramental

put on your robes
and wash your hands
before you touch
the body and the blood
of all this love
bathe the air
in incense
pour the wine
and wind your words
in tapestries around the bed
and answer
     yes, I am the celebrant

the women

I fear
the flood
of careless rhythm
in their walk
fear too
the unctuous cadence
of their voice

for they will be to him
asphalt
to the sun

falling—again

my heart
a kiddie's carousel
revolves
in undulating flow
along a predetermined course
anticipating
the syncopated rise and fall
of the monkey-organ

until some fleeting gesture
movement
word
touches the blindest center deep in me
and I am powerless to stop the sudden rush
the rising thrust
that closes like a manacle around my chest
and clouds my eyes

crashing

love
is an ego-trip
across the peaks and craters of my womanhood
a weightless flight from self
into the sun-hot mirror of your eyes
where quickening lakes and springs enflame the skin
and sudden softnesses renew the after-glow of all my suns
and move the liquid mass of dormant me

in the shattering glass
I see
only myself
in you

ace-man

handing you the pack
I curl into my corner
waiting

you take the lead
dealing quick and sure
then make your bid
spreading the deck
face-up
across the table

no gambling now

my kings and queens
are paper dolls
beneath your gaze

the ace
your aching clarity

gemini

your manliness
envelopes me
and fills my eyes

I glance away

then
turning
face suddenly
the child in you

easy come

among talk of marinas
and motor-house boats
your eyes
hold mine

I know I want you
for the hell of it

marinas aren't my style
but
oh
you are

Caribbean exile

you played their game
mastering
the strange arrhythmic rules
with deceptive ease
scoring every sub-goal
with a cool precision

your real goal out of reach
on a ridge of mountain
bathed in salt
and sand
and sun-hot
wrapped in green and gold
and a rush of foaming white
against the blue blue endless ocean
of yourself

and still you play
circling
aiming
winning
within the cold rectangle
of white-lime
on a frozen ground

looking all the while
over your shoulder
at the rock

you, Mercutio!

you told me
life was love
and love a vague
and visionary thing
yet absolute

in love meant
only you, for me, for ever
long before I knew
what you, or me, or ever
meant

now, meaningless
your words rise up
from ashes of old loves
burnt out
so many phoenixes

once more I meet the time
for making
shaping
love
this time
I'll mould his feet of clay

(but love hath wings, Mercutio!)

ah love!
then soar above me
in your flight
and leave me free
to walk the earth
without you

parting

you speak the truths
I cannot say
and
waiting in the dark
receive only
in return
my silence
a deafening consent

leaving home

I have no quarrel
with the smell of fruits soaked
in rum and cherry wine
the brilliant one-day bloom
victorious yellow
at the gate
or the blood-red
of a thousand sudden cherries
on the tree

but if I let the ivy
start
I may have to wait forever
while it climbs
and clings
and winds its way
along the garden wall

love in the lotus

someday
lovingly
gladly
and at last
we'll explore asanas
exchange mantras
and
my long-legged guru
remember
that the lotus
is basic

hearts of glass

build me
a modern house
with walls of glass
that let the sun
shine in

that let my eyes
dissolve
the bars of love
and show you
in

lend me
your heart of glass
and I will turn it
round
toward the light

and
defenseless
see
the me
in you

lovers
in glass houses
throw no stones

ℬ

Kilimanjaro

the densely packed quadrangle
at the Kilimanjaro
is jammed with faces

amidst layers of black on brown
a pair of piercing eyes
beneath a shiny oval bald patch
appear at my side, offering a bribe
a beer for a dance
he says, in an accent I do not recognize
only if you are a good dancer
I reply

as we move into the music
I see that I am in expert hands
a partner dancer
he is synchrony or nothing

mouths pressed against each other's ears
we shout our names and birth places
Haiti—Jamaica
but the music knows no borders
as the voices of the diaspora slide
from English patwas of the Caribbean
to French creoles from Haiti to the Seychelles
and cross the vast continent in all its vibrance
we do not have to miss a beat
our bodies speak one language—
soca, makossa, soukous, kompa, zouk, reggae—
the rhythms are ours
spawned in the long river of Africa
wrapped halfway around the world

on the deep pulse of the reggae
he is a fraction too fast
moving just ahead of the bass
on the music of our American brothers
we head for the bar
he is way too fluid for the sharp angularity
of this side of the ocean

he buys me a beer
and massages my feet under the table

sometime in the night the rhythm slows
and as his lips brush mine I know
that his kiss will fit into my mouth
like a child's mouth on a mango

a tall man in a suit
dancing a smooth salsa next to us
touches him on the shoulder
and signals with a tilt of his head
that he is about to leave
>   my cousin has to go now
>   if I stay, will you drop me home?

later
in a café—bookstore on Connecticut Avenue
he pulls a thin paperback from a cluttered shelf
"The Little Prince", he says
and offers to buy it for me if I have five dollars

across the small wrought iron table
and the heavily sugared espresso
that stand between us
he reads slowly
puckered vowels wrapping softly around non-existant r's
it is only with the heart that one can see rightly
what is essential is invisible to the eye

sometime after four
we stop at his house to get his cousin's car
and he asks me to come in—to see where he lives—
but his real intention is to introduce himself to me
by showing me his family

rifling through a box of photographs
he deals them to me one by one—
a formal oval portrait in black and white shows his mother
light brown and lady-like
beside the clean, hard darkness of her husband
his careful education shining sharply
through the same intense black eyes he has passed on to his son—
a young woman with thick braids resting on her shoulders—
a glowing two year old in soft focus—
and numerous cousins, the result, he says
of his grandfather's very busy zozo

in the cool air of early morning he walks me to my car
I give him a card with my phone number
and he offers in return a handful of cassettes
here, these will keep you awake on your way home
he drives ahead, leading me to the highway
then waves me on

the light gray of morning stands ahead of me
as the sweet drums start in my ears
the language, I surmise, must be Haitian Creole
but the message is familiar
I do not need to know the words

I have met a man who dances
for the sake of synchrony
buys me a book with my own money
reads to me of seeing with the heart
takes me to his home at dawn to show me pictures
of his parents, his child, his ex-wife
and blames innumerable cousins on the busy-ness
of his grandfather's zozo

I arrive home
and there is a message on my phone
just calling to make sure you got home safely

morning has broken

OCEAN NIGHTS

Melanie

little girl
you blew my world apart
when you appeared
defying
with your intense fragility
my clean-cut classic image
of motherhood

but when you fixed those bright black
ackee-eyes on me
and clutched my heart with all your might
I knew
that it was sink or swim
for both of us

and so it was we swam against the tide
at one in strength and one in inspiration

until you died
and blew my world apart
again

for Mark, at seven

with all the power
of your growing self
you stand
alone
an entity apart

how can it be
that
because I am your mother
I must hold your happiness
in my hand?

dream child

who is this child
that lives
inside my dreams?

sometimes
my own
my beautiful
my son

or then
some prodigy
precocious
to a fault

or now
a faceless bundle
of dependent infancy

always
the breath of danger
in the air
a child imperiled
by his own power
or by encircling arms
that stifle him

or is it you
my sweet
who haunts me still?
in sleek disguise
the many selves
you might have been

a visit from my father

Sunday afternoon
and you arrive
gaunt limping shadow
of my childhood's sun
the life-lines deeper drawn
along your face
the light of knowledge
in your eyes

touching my cheek
you say
that you have come
to see my house
and, with stumbling paces
you explore the territory

as wooden beams reveal
a marked asymmetry
you sense the something wrong
    where is the child?
you ask
hurrying inside

finding the woman curled beneath the bed
child to her breast
you challenge her
    but here she is
    I thought you said that she was lost

it is my voice that rises from the dust
    not this one, Daddy,
    the other one was here
    I only turned my back and she is gone

invitation

the brightest sea
I ever saw
deep-circling blue
within a bay
and opening wide
to rolling ocean
and unending view

    here is the spot for which we searched
    said I to my shadow

      what perils lurk in those dark depths?
      no matter that the sands are clear
      their luster blinds
      their charm beguiles
      we are safer here

I saw the enchanting promise
my shadow saw the threat
remembering she lacked my skill
in swimming
I acquiesced

dream climbing

tonight I climb the endless scaffolding
that reaches up and up
through layers of night sky
to god-knows-where
the rhythm easy in my limbs
I grasp
then climb
then reach and grasp again
I have no fear
of this bold enterprise

below
the ever-present shadow follows me
and, weary with the climb
she rests her infant's cradle
on a ledge of iron at her side

one arm outstretched
to help her up
I lean into the dark

she grips my hand
and
we are locked in terror
as the little cot turns
tumbling
for never-ending moments
through the night

descending hurriedly
she fades away from me
until
detached and powerless
on the top-most rung
I watch
distant scurrying figures
burying their dead

B'

ocean night

and now
the sea rolls through my night
relentlessly

in waves of rushing brown
that roar and crash along the open beach
on which you flaunt your power and your innocence

for it is you they want
my free and fearless boy
you are their victim
and their prize
and in the blackness of a moment
you are gone

as I search for you
I tell myself
this time
I'll let the scream engulf me
raise my arms
and let the pain release me
no holding back
no reasoning
this time

but as the flood begins
I feel a warm small body
at my side
and your imperious waking
calls me into morning

underworld

the hounds return
to haunt me

as massive blackness heaves
across the terrain
of my dreams
urgent hands
pull at the bolts
and slam the padlocks in

they surge toward the gate

then spill
in shapeless bulk
beneath
above
between
the iron bars
(no barriers these)

I cower
wrestling
with the manacle of sleep
and scream
for consciousness

drums for Kenny

the drumming stopped
at midnight

twelve hours
of young hands battering
against the tightly stretched
goat-skins
telling the world
that Kenny was dead
and his friends had come
to beat some drums
for him

and Esdelle
in his hopeful
nine-year-old grief
wailing

now I think the whole world
will hear about this!

the recipe

here I stand
expert cracker of eggs
tapping gently
on the sharp ceramic edge

with a measured turn of wrist
the shiny yellow circles
slide cleanly
from their bed of viscous white
a tidy separation of the parts
according to the recipe
at hand

but staring in dismay
I see my utmost care
result
in the untidiest of ends

and I must spend
the balance of the dream
fingers slipping
on its elusive slime
and crumbling shell

Mr. Pickersgown

hello again my buttoned-down lover
tucked neatly into the pocket of my day-time jeans
like the fantasy companion of my childhood play
wherein a little girl incarcerates her love
until it's time for tea
       you may come out now, Mr. Pickersgown
(everything in its place and nothing before time
you see)

but when I sleep
you easily escape the jailor's key
and weave your way
throughout the loosened fabric of my dreams
forever smiling
and forever young

transformed sometimes
into a jaunty fireman doll in scarlet truck and suit
waving goodbye
or then an artless teenaged youth with open arms
hurrying toward me
at some midnight rendezvous

now
high on a hill
a gentle stranger
studying the inscription
on a paper pendant
hung around my neck
asks who is my lover

it is a stranger's face
but the eyes are yours

sonnet

Is not the sea life's greatest parallel?
Do not it's mighty waves strike home a truth
That shatters all the confidence of youth
That tears the ego from its ivory cell
And casts it headlong through the caves of hell
Where mortal dreams lie idle and uncouth
And every thought a narrow, childish youth
Of no significance? For in the swell
Of this vast ocean, we are swept along
Unnoticed in one wave, forever growing
And ignoring all it passes on its way.
Nor will it stop at the request
Of one who seeks to save some dream
That soon must lie beyond recall

EDEN

eden

not by bread alone my joy shall be
nor to man alone my constancy
with fowl of air and fish of sea
with worm and beast and flower and tree
shall my dominion be

let fire burn my too hard bone
and oil anoint my too dry skin
let air and earth my constant cohorts be
in Heraclitean flux defy
my immobility

and when by sun alone my eyes shall see
untouched by earth and sky and sea
to elemental heights no longer free
I shall
from dust to dust
consign my anonymity

island apocalypse

power stone
key stone
dry and cool from earth belly
smooth and hard from river bed
bring your power down

thunder stone
fire stone
strong white rum will catch your flame
sweet olive oil will slake your thirst
crushed mango bark with gully root
wild plantain leaf and obi seed
will feed your power now

power stone
key stone
warm sheepblood will give you life
goat headbone will keep you strong
old cockhead and young bullseed
and fresh cut heart of morocoy
will free your power now

when fire melt your sacrifice
and blood and bush and stone is one
then stand in sun-hot
warm
blood warm
and call your power down

power stone: ritual object holding spiritual power in Afro-Caribbean religions

the rivermaids

my black Eurydice
skin of velvet
coal-black
now shadowless
assails me with blank eyes
and thighs of stone
her soul beyond the power
of sacrificial blood
and balm-yard bath
her body, death-in-life
tied to my hand

while I, some reincarnate Orpheus
kneel to young waters
at the river's head
and proclaim to semi-human powers
from an alien element
my now weak humanness
until my tongue
dry as april grass
can move no more

I leave their bank
gaze riveted ahead
(with one false flick of eye
I lose my love to them)
until her shadow
lies on the earth
and the deathly flesh
tied to my own
is born again

ℛ

rivermaid: mythological water spirit of Tobago

mermaid

she lives only
in the sweet river
of her woman-self

deny her this
and
gasping
she flounders on the bank
the vista blurred
before unfocussed eyes
yearning
the slow seeping flood
of self
through saturated skin
and love-soaked pores

but she must learn
to breathe
the air
for in the tropic blaze
her chosen element
evaporates
beneath the sun

sestina

the poor-house coolie-man says he remembers
the day when the river
came down, the shift of thick black
mud on the banks, and twisted
coconut-boughs—his memory
stretches that far

but beyond that, he says, is too far
for an old man's mind to go—as a river
surrenders all memory
of self to the sea, and abandons its twisted
land-life, so, he insists, the black
of that morning's flood is all that he remembers

if asked of the woman, he remembers
no woman, at least, none with the cool black
skin we describe—nothing but a heavy river
in spate—that was all—nor a child with a twisted
leg—his feeble old mind cannot travel so far
but it was all the same day, she must be part of that memory

now, he says, how can a poor-house memory
keep track of all the black
women who slept on and off under the twisted
frames of the coolie shacks? her body lay at the far
end of the settlement, but he remembers
only the ugly haste of the river

her child was born near the river
bank, with a lame leg and the straight black
hair of a coolie-child—no matter how far
removed the time, an old man's memory
should know of a lame cross-breed? but he remembers
only that all their lives were twisted

there is always shame in a twisted
birth—what should he know of such things? the surging river
meant death for the ragged shacks and all memory
of the life within them. after that day he went far
from the camp and now only remembers
that both water and women were black

outside the poor-house memory a thin black
girl taps a twisted leg impatiently, waiting till he remembers
more about the far-off rage of the river

sensay time

if your excrement is wormy
your intestine somewhat squirmy
if your urine turns out germy
you'll agree
to cabbage bark and vervine
velvet bush and tamarind
senna and cerasee
in a tureen of bush tea

if you find yourself ill-mated
and your appetite is sated
your blood pressure escalated
into wrath
crushed love-bush and avocado
white cho-cho and banana
and strong Jamaican quassia
make a wonderful bush-bath

if your love is unrequited
or by neighbors you are slighted
or a great career is blighted—
for a fee
some juice of ramgoat roses
milk of sulphur with bluestone
is fried in secret workings
to make your oil of set-me-free

but just take my word now brother
don't wait for the balm-yard mother
you can save yourself the bother
of her creed
for you won't need her ever
if you daily rediscover
the joys of cannabis sativa
the good old wisdom weed

sensay: Jamaican term for marijuana

the bargain

Anansi
smart-man
sam-fi-man
head-man

     listen
     I need you
     the whiteman is after my arse

     see me here
Anansi

     dry-tongue, breath coming hard
     my heart, the drummer's hand gone wild,
     battering my chest
     and fear making knots in my belly

friend
my friend

     hear me
     study your head
     spin out a web
     soft and strong like my woman's thigh
     shiny and soft to catch the sun
     let it warm and glow
     grow a web
Anansi

     to fatten the whiteman's eye
brother
brother-man

     you know me
     you know I'm a man with sons
     and land
     and a woman

     and you know my daughter
Anansi

     a sweet girl-child
     soft and ripe
     like a morning plum
Br'Anancy

     you know me man!

B

Anansi/Br'Anancy: West African spider trickster hero

wata mumma

wata mumma oi!
wata!
wata mumma!

     wata mumma, bwoy?

wata, ma!
de pickney was a play eena Fada Tayla yard
an a Gladys tun fi ketch
an im han slip
an de ball dis fly go up eena Fada mango tree
an a fat, fat mango drop!
an—

     drop, bwoy?

drop—buff—ma!
an Gladys tell dem say
     mmhn now, a no fi wi, so oonoo lef de mango yah!
an Lesta laugh an say
     ef mango drop a groung
     a no fi Fada Tayla
     an a no fi oonoo own
     a fi dutti own
     an sence mi dutti too
     a fi mi!
but as Lesta stretch im han—
whissh!
lickle mos Fada Tayla tambran switch
chop it gawn!
an all weh Lesta run and bawl
     a no me, Fada, no me sah!
de tambran like a lightnin still a chop cross Lesta head
so Lesta jump barb wire fence top-side Miss Mattie yard
an drop dung a de groung
an roll dung big big hillside go a gully
an—

gully bwoy?

gully, ma! dry gully!
an as Lesta li dung sof eena dry dry gully bed
Fada stan up pon de hillside wid nine lime eena im han
an im a bawl
　　　yu no know sey gully no good fi tief, Lesta?
an Lesta laugh and say
　　　mi no tief, sah! an ol man can roll come dung a gully!
same time Fada hol de lime eena im han
an—

　　　lime, bwoy?

nine lime, ma!
im hol de lime eena im han
an wine im han so tell me tink it a go fly off a im back
an same time lime a fly go dung a gully and drop—buff—
top-side a Lesta head
but Lesta—im no badda fi look back
im dis a roll an laugh
so im no see de wata dis a jump up from de gully
an—

　　　wata, bwoy?

wata from the dry dry gully, ma!
de same place wey de lime dem drop
wata come
an Lesta im a roll and laugh an laugh an roll
an im no see sey every roll im roll one lime a drop
an every drop it drop mo wata baan
an wata dis a come up back a Lesta
till it start fi roll dung gully bed
and come a Lesta foot!
an time Lesta look and see wha a go on
an start fi bawl and jump
de wata de a im belly
an im a flap an bawl like senseh fowl
　　　mumma! mumma! mi mumma oi!
an Fada dis a bawl back
　　　a wha mek yu a bawl fi mumma, Lesta!
　　　a no fi yu mumma dat

a wata mumma bwoy!

wata mumma, bwoy?

wata mumma, ma!

whooay!
wata!
wata mumma oi!
wata mumma de pon Lesta
        whaioi!
        wata mumma drink up Lesta
        oonoo run go dung a gully
        fi go see if Lesta drownded
        eena wata mumma belly!
                belly oi!
                        wataaa!
                        belly!
                                mummaaa
                                        wata mumma
                                                wata

mummaaaa!

ℬ

wata mumma/wata mammy: mythological Jamaican water spirit with control
over the sea, rivers, and dry river beds or "gullies"